Anxiety Sucks:
Teen Survival Guide

Natasha Daniels, LCSW

DEDICATION

To my three children who continue to teach me more about life than anyone else I know and to my husband who ensures I will have at least one hearty laugh each day!

CONTENTS

ACKNOWLEDGMENTS

This book couldn't have been written without the help and insight from the children and teens I have met in my therapy practice. I have met many anxiety warriors that have shown such bravery, fortitude and humor in the face of adversity.

INTRODUCTION

This book is intended for informational purposes only and does not replace the guidance and support of a mental health professional. Therapists offer personalized support, insight and guidance that a book cannot. Arm yourself with skills, but consider getting a therapist as your co-pilot.

This book is purposely short and can be read in one sitting. It is meant to arm you with skills that you can use right away. As you practice these skills, re-read the book for motivation and encouragement. You can do this!

Was this book thrown at you? Did someone plead with you to read it? Or are you desperately searching for help, looking for your *own* solutions? Either way, you have come to the right place.

Anxiety sucks.

It does. I am not going to paint a pretty picture for you. From nausea and vomiting to horrible and scary thoughts—it's not fun.

Trust me, I know. I was a kid who was convinced someone was breaking into my house each night. I was a kid whose stomach hurt so badly from nerves I constantly feared I would throw up. I was a kid who entered college and not only acquired an education but acquired lovely panic attacks as well.

I got angry. Really angry. I wasn't going to let this monster ruin my life. I struggled alone and I kicked its butt alone. I could have used the help. I could have tackled the issue sooner—but no one taught me how.

I now have a pretty cool job. I get to help other kids slay their anxiety beast and teach them how to end their suffering much sooner than I was able to end mine.

I have made this book short. You're welcome. You don't need to read a novel to beat anxiety. I will give you the lowdown, teach you mad skills and send you on your happy way.

Deal?

Now let's stop this chit chat and kick some anxiety butt.

1 WHO IS THIS BEAST YOU CALL *ANXIETY?*

Let's start with the cast of characters in this story. First, we have the star of the show—that would be you. Take a bow. And we have your co-star—not to be outdone—Anxiety.

I would like to refer to your co-star with a name more fitting for his role. Perhaps Little Dictator would work or when he's really annoying we can call him Dic. Hey, you gotta have some humor through this mess!

So how did you acquire this annoying companion? Unfortunately, you have your parents to blame or at least their DNA. You see anxiety has a strong genetic component. So just as you might have inherited your Aunt Kate's beautiful green eyes, you might have gotten her anxiety as well. I know; that sucks.

But before you go cursing out your aunt (or whoever passed down those beautiful genes) you should know that anxiety comes with some pretty cool side dishes. Anxious people tend to be extremely kindhearted, considerate and trustworthy. They are often more sensitive and in touch with other people's emotions. They tend to be deep thinkers and great planners. Nothing is going to catch them off guard. These traits make them great friends, relatives, students and employees. Now, enough of the ego stroking!

The bottom line is *you* are pretty awesome. Your little dictator is not.

Your little dictator has always been there. Maybe you didn't notice him when you were little. He is pretty good at hiding—but more than likely you were born with him.

It was just a matter of time until your dictator made his first entrance onto the scene. He was always written into the script. Lots of people think their anxiety was caused by something. Maybe you think it was because you saw someone throw up at school or the time you had a nasty stomach virus. Maybe it was because of something you watched or read. But in reality, it was most likely none of those things. Your dictator was waiting to join the show—he just needed an introduction.

The good news is ultimately you get to write the script. Do you want your dictator to have a big role or a small role? Spoiler alert—he likes to steal the show. And if you are reading this he has probably been doing a pretty good job of it so far. But don't worry—that, my friend, is all about to change.

You are not alone.

So you might be thinking, *So great, this lady is telling me I was born with this bizarre dictator in my brain that follows me around and makes my life miserable!* Well, metaphorically, yes. Obviously, you don't have a real dictator in your brain but it can sure feel that way sometimes. But it is not all doom and gloom. We are all born with various struggles, yours just happens to be anxiety. The good news is you can defeat this metaphorical little man, I will show you how.

You are not alone. Roughly 1 out of 4 kids will struggle with anxiety. You might think, *Yeah right*! But it's true. People with anxiety don't go around with a billboard advertising their anxiety. Most people—*you* probably included—suffer silently.

How does your dictator operate?

I like to think of your dictator as an annoying, paranoid companion. He sits on your shoulder constantly looking out for danger. The only problem is he is really bad at it. He completely overreacts and he makes you overreact too. Worse—not only does he have access to your mind, the little dude has access to your body as well. So when this paranoid bundle of misery thinks you're in danger, he hits the emergency alarm and prepares you for war. A war that isn't happening.

When he activates the alarm, he throws your body into chaos. Your body thinks it needs to prepare you for battle. Maybe you have heard of the fight or flight response in biology? That's what's happening to your body.

Your body is preparing to fight. Your heart starts to race giving you an extra boost in case you need to run for your life. Your body moves all of its energy away from unnecessary activities such as digestion— causing nausea, constipation and diarrhea. It floods adrenaline throughout you giving you super strength—along with dizziness and headaches. All this activity can cause chest pain, shortness of breath and most of all panic! All in an effort to keep you safe.

The worst part about this whole disaster is that the pain is real. It is not in your head, it is in your body. But it was your dictator that triggered this mess. Like a guilty kid who accidentally broke something, the dictator tries to cover up his mess. He tells you, "Wow! Something bad must be happening, why else would you be feeling this way?" He tries to convince you there is something medically wrong with you. "Maybe you are having a heart attack. Maybe there is something seriously wrong with you. You should freak out!" No—the reality is your dictator caused it and he doesn't want to own up to what he did.

Eventually, your brain realizes that it's been scammed *again* and it starts to power down, all the while leaving you confused and exhausted.

What happens when you buddy up with your dictator?

Lots of people buddy up with their dictator. Most people won't admit it but they do. They make a nice, cozy spot for him in their brain and constantly feed him, keeping him strong. Why would someone do that? Because he is like an annoying two-year-old. He is constantly nagging people and wearing them down. Sometimes it is just easier to give him what he wants. You don't want me to go to the party? Fine, I will find a way to avoid it. You don't want me to go to school? Fine, just leave me alone and I won't go.

The scary reality is that your dictator has some mad skills! He is very shifty and he can convince you that *you* don't want to do these things. He'll convince you it has nothing to do with him or anxiety!

- You don't want to go to school because you're sick. *Not* because you are worried.

- You don't want to go to the party because it sounds boring. *Not* because you are afraid to talk to people.

- You wash your hands all the time because they are dirty. *Not* because you are afraid of getting sick.

Your dictator doesn't want you to know that he has the remote control to your brain. He doesn't want you to realize that he is the one calling the shots, wreaking havoc on your body and mind. In a perfect world he would like to be completely invisible, completely off your radar—living a life of anonymity.

When you deny he exists, he revels in your ignorance. When you make excuses for his behavior, he thinks you're awesome. All the while he's growing bigger and bossier, dictating what you should do and how you should think. That's not cool.

Why taking your little man down is the only option.

You might have a soft spot for your dictator but, trust me; he is not your friend. When you provide a nice, cozy place for him, he likes it. When you believe all of his lies, he loves you. When you follow his irrational demands, he gets fed. When he gets fed, he gets bigger. When he gets bigger, he gets louder and more paranoid. And that, my friend, is not good news for you.

You don't need to politely tell your dictator to leave you alone. You need to annihilate him. He doesn't get the hint. He doesn't take no for an answer. It is either him or you. You are either going to live your life according to his fears or you'll have to obliterate him.

Anxiety Themes.

Not all dictators are the same. They come in all different shapes and sizes. Some are giants and some are little pests. His size is ultimately up to you. You can feed him and grow him big or starve him and make him small.

Your dictator loves to study you. He studies your fears, your doubts. He is your silent companion through life watching your reactions and scanning your thoughts for insecurities.

What does your dictator do with his findings? He hones in on your weak spots. He learns where you are most vulnerable and makes his plan of attack. Usually your dictator will pick one or two areas where he can get to you the most. I like to call these areas anxiety themes.

It is important to try to figure out what type of anxiety themes your dictator is trying to sell you. Once you know what he is trying to sell you'll know exactly what not to buy!

So let's reveal the most common anxiety themes and take the power away from your dictator. Some of these themes will sound very,

very familiar while other themes might sound completely foreign to you. Usually people only have a few themes.

Here are some of the horrible thoughts your dictator might be trying to sell you:

You are going to get a disease and die.

Yup. He'll tell you that you are not safe from germs. They are lurking around every corner, on every doorknob and on every switch. People are just human incubators carrying germs—waiting to infect you.

But wait, that's not all. Is that a lump on your head? A weird, brown spot on your arm? Could it be cancer? Maybe a tumor? Maybe you should go online and check. Are you feeling hot? Do you have a fever? Maybe you should check to see if you have a temperature.

Is that plant food you just touched poisonous? Is that bug spray safe? What if some of that sunscreen got in your mouth—should you go to the hospital?

If it's all about your health, this is your theme.

You have to be perfect.

Getting anything under an A is not acceptable. Success means perfection—there is no in between. Failure is not an option. You stay up late worrying about projects and exams only to ace them. But that's not good enough for you. You scrutinize your grade. Why the minus, why not an A+? You compare yourself to others. The boy behind you scored one point higher than you. Why did that happen? You are not the smartest or the best. You are a failure.

Because you are so hard on yourself you might have test anxiety. You might feel sick or lightheaded during an exam. You might blank out and forget everything you have learned. You might feel sick to your stomach the night before testing and have a hard time going to school.

If only this perfectionism ended with your school work. Usually it oozes into every aspect of your life. The teacher yelled at the boy sitting next to you. Was she yelling at you too? She told the class to stop goofing off. Was that comment directed at you? Does she hate you?

Don't naively think you can leave the school building and be done with this theme. Do you play sports or an instrument? Your high standards follow you wherever you go. Did you miss that pass? Did you not run as fast as your teammates? Did you run .5 seconds slower than the fastest runner? What a complete failure!

If you strive for perfectionism in everything you do, this is your theme.

Everyone is judging you.

You take self-consciousness to another level. You feel like everyone is always staring at you. Watching you. Judging you. You got a new haircut—everyone will laugh. You are sporting a new pimple—everyone will point. There is very little that won't embarrass you.

You may become socially withdrawn because you are so hyper focused on how people view you. You are constantly feeling left out— even though, in reality, it probably isn't happening the way you perceive it. You feel like you have no good friends but you have pretty high standards when it comes to how you define a "good" friend.

Your fear of being judged can cause you some major problems. You aren't quick to talk to others out of fear of being rejected. Because of this fear big social gatherings might upset you. You might find yourself avoiding pretty much any situation that has the potential to make you feel socially awkward. Your family might nag you to go out and "have some fun." They don't realize that just the idea of going out with other people gives you heart palpitations.

It sucks to constantly worry about what other people think. It can make you re-play a conversation over and over again in your head. It can keep you up all night wringing your hands about a class presentation. It can make you avoid the awkwardness of a phone call or a video chat. It can even make it hard to order your own food or talk to strangers.

When you are consumed with how other people view you, this is your theme.

You are not safe.

Danger lurks around every corner. When it gets dark no one is safe. You are constantly thinking about how people can break in and hurt you. What would you do? Do you have an escape plan or a makeshift weapon to yield in case of an emergency?

You are a master of *what ifs*. What if we get into a car accident? What if the plane crashes? What if lightning sets our house on fire?

What if I get bitten by a spider?

The *what ifs* are endless—as are your worries.

If you can think of all the ways you are not safe, this is your theme.

You are not okay unless you are with your mom.

You know it doesn't make sense but you don't feel okay unless you are with your mom. Maybe you worry about her safety, maybe you worry about your safety, but unless you are together you are feeling panicky. Where did she go? When will she be back? How long will she be gone? It is as if you have an invisible string keeping you attached.

You are constantly evaluating who your mom is with and what she is doing. Can she get hurt doing that? You have an irrational belief that as long as you are with her nothing bad can happen.

You might worry more about your own safety. You depend on your mom to keep you safe and you feel vulnerable when she is not with you. You count the hours and minutes until you will see your mom again. Maybe you text her multiple times a day. Maybe you can't get through the whole school day without bailing and going home.

If this is your worry, don't be embarrassed. It is actually a common theme and has nothing to do with maturity or age. Sometimes this dependency transfers over to your partner or your own children as you get older. Don't worry; we are going to crush this thing before it gets that far.

If you keep tabs on where your mom is, this is your theme.

You are going to throw up in front of other people.

This may have started when you got sick in public or when you witnessed someone else throwing up; however, you may have had none of these experiences but still have this theme. This is one of the dictator's favorite themes. It is convenient because, as we talked about earlier, anxiety can make you feel nauseous. When you feel nauseous all the time you naturally worry about throwing up. This worry can start to consume you. What if I throw up in class? What if I throw up at lunch? What if I throw up at the party? Maybe I should just stay home.

Unfortunately, this is a vicious cycle. The more you worry about throwing up the more nauseous you get. The more nauseous you get the more you worry about throwing up. It is a cruel theme.

If you are constantly worrying about throwing up, this is your theme.

You are going to have a panic attack in front of other people.

You've experienced the dreaded panic attack. They are not fun. I am sure you agree. You agree so much that you will do everything in your power to avoid that feeling again. You are convinced that home is a safer place than anywhere else. It is home base. Leaving home makes you feel vulnerable. What if I have a panic attack? What will I do? How long will it take me to get back home? You base everything in your life on how far it is from your home and how long it will take you to get back.

If you worry about having a panic attack in public, this is your theme.

You will never be happy with your appearance.

Your nose is too big. You are too fat. Your thighs are too wide. You are too tall or too short. You are constantly obsessed with your appearance. Everyone tells you not to worry about it—that you look great—but no one can convince you otherwise. Most teens worry about their looks but your looks *consume* you. You spend hours getting ready in the morning. You have missed school because you didn't look your best. You take physical insecurity to another level—it is an obsession, an obsession that makes you miserable, makes you worry.

If you are consumed with unhappiness because of your appearance, this is your theme.

***

Okay, that should give you a pretty good picture of some of the anxiety themes out there. There are more, but we don't have all day. I promised to keep this short.

Did you find yourself in some of those descriptions? Now that you might know what themes you have you'll be aware of the type of worries your dictator will try to sell you.

Up next... I will reveal the secret inner workings of your little dictator. Let's expose him and his scams.

2 YOUR DICTATOR'S TACTICS

So how does this whole anxiety thing work? Well, unfortunately, your dictator has some pretty covert operations. He really doesn't want to get caught and he doesn't want you to build a defense against him. His work is slow and methodical. But don't worry; I've been infiltrating him for some time and know all of his moves.

Throughout this book we'll be following the lives and struggles of Tami, Jon and Amanda, three people with three very different anxiety themes. They actually represent hundreds of people I have worked with over the years rolled into these three composite characters. For the sake of simplicity, I have focused on only one worry for each of them. Most people will have many worries under their anxiety theme—and may even have several anxiety themes.

Let's stroll with them for a bit and see how all of their dictators operate.

Let me introduce you to Tami. Tami is a typical sixteen-year-old girl. She is a good student and has some great friends. If you asked anyone they would say Tami is a friendly, likable girl. But Tami has a secret. She is overwhelmed with anxiety. It takes everything out of her just to go to school. Her friends don't know. Her teachers don't know. She keeps her struggles to herself. The only people who are aware of her struggles are her parents. The same people who drag her out of bed, plead with her to get dressed and force her to go to school.

Tami is consumed with fear. She worries non-stop that she is going to throw up. She can't remember when it began—maybe in 5th grade when this boy Jacob barfed in the cafeteria or maybe on that road trip when she felt car sick. Whatever it was it hasn't gone away.

***

Meet Jon. Jon is a fourteen-year-old boy. Most kids in Jon's class wouldn't recognize him if he was walking down the street. He is the quiet boy hugging the back wall of the classroom. He keeps to himself as much as he can. You might not think much of him but he thinks a lot about you. He is a quiet observer. In fact, that is his biggest problem. He constantly feels like people are staring at him, judging him. He overanalyzes every glance, every conversation and replays it again and again in his head.

As you might have guessed, Jon is deathly afraid of talking in front of the class. He worries his teachers will call on him. He worries about looking foolish. He worries about doing class presentations. He would prefer to be home schooled. He feels exhausted by the end of the day.

***

And, finally, we have Amanda. Amanda has had worries since as long as she can remember. From monsters and zombies to aliens and bad guys, she continually has fears. Her biggest fears come out at night. She has a hard time sleeping. She thought she'd outgrow it but she is now seventeen years old with no end in sight. At night, she hears every creak and bump. She is constantly convinced that a bad guy has broken into her home.

Daytime isn't much better. She worries about her safety and of potential dangers. Will they get into a car accident? Is it going to rain? Will it flood the house? Will she choke? Will she get a disease and die? When everyone else is excited about the family vacation, her mind is fixated on the flight. Will they crash? Will she feel sick?

She hoped school would be a break from all these worries but it just adds to them. Will someone get angry and shoot up the school? Will a madman with a weapon come on campus? Will a tornado hit the school so she won't be able to find her way home?

Amanda constantly lives in *What If* land and she doesn't know how to get out.

***

So there's some background. Three people with three very different worries but with one thing in common—they all have a dictator, a dictator that plots and plans how to keep these worries alive, how to keep them all feeling miserable. Who needs that?

Here is the breakdown of how dictators work:

Step 1: Plant the seeds of doubt.

Your dictator is your front seat passenger. He is constantly with you giving you his two cents. His first step is to wear you down. He is the negative voice in your head constantly nagging you in the background. If he can just plant the seeds of doubt within you his master plan will work.

Let's take a look at how this usually goes down with our new compadres Tami, Jon and Amanda.

Tami promised her mom that she would make an effort to go to school. She has missed a ridiculous amount of days and the school sent a letter home warning her of her frequent absences. Tami and her mom made an agreement that she would try harder. Tami thought to herself, *How much harder can I try*? but agreed.

She woke up in a good mood. Her class was having a special event that day and she was excited to be part of it. The night before she even put out her favorite outfit to wear. Her mom was impressed that she was making such an effort. She was going to do this. Nothing would stop her. She started to get dressed...

And then the dictator started planting the seeds of doubt.

Ooh, does your stomach hurt? I think your stomach hurts.

No, I feel fine.

What if you feel fine now but once you get to school you feel nauseous?

I feel fine.

That would be so embarrassing to throw up in front of everyone. Today's assembly is in the auditorium—everyone will see you.

That would be embarrassing.

If you throw up you'll have nowhere to go. Everyone will be so grossed out.

That would suck.

I think your stomach hurts. Don't you?

It actually does a bit now that I think about it.

Are you sure you want to risk it and go to school? Is it worth that much embarrassment?

Not really.

Good. Go tell your mom you feel too sick to go.

And so it begins.

***

Jon had a class presentation. He had been nervous about it all week. He thought about pretending to be sick but he knew it would just delay the inevitable. He was well prepared. He had note cards with everything he needed to say. He had practiced his speech three times in front of his brother. He knew his stuff. An hour before the presentation he was able to convince himself that he could do this. He had nothing to worry about. He watched the first person go. He watched the second person go.

And then the dictator entered the scene...

Yours isn't as good as theirs.

Mine is pretty good.

Take a look around the room. Everyone is staring at the presenter.

Yup. That's what they are supposed to do.

They are going to laugh so hard at your presentation.

No they won't.

Sarah, that girl you think is cute—she's going to see you turn bright red.

That would be embarrassing.

She'll never want to talk to you after today.

I would look like a loser.

Everyone will talk about the kid who turned bright red in history class.

I won't want to ever come back to school.

You don't need to do this. You can be creative, come up with an excuse.

I don't want to do this!

Damage done.

***

Amanda was exhausted. She hadn't had a good night's sleep in so long. She convinced herself that tonight would be different. No more restless nights. She was safe. She had nothing to worry about. She snuggled into bed. She put her closet light on so her room wasn't pitch black. She wished she could just relax. Things started off well. She was tired. She thought about her day and what she needed to do tomorrow. She was about to pat herself on the back about how relaxed she felt until—

The dictator started to point things out...

Did you just hear the floorboards creak? It kind of sounded like someone is walking down the hall.

I didn't hear anything.

Listen closer! Doesn't it sound like someone is walking out there?

I can't hear anything.

I think there is someone standing right in front of your door!

I can't hear anything.

Of course you can't. They are trying to be quiet now. They know you heard them.

Yikes! What should I do if they open the door?

You are not safe. It is just a matter of seconds until that door bursts open.

My heart is pounding so fast!

Dictator's work complete.

Step 2: And now for your feature film of everything that can go wrong.

Step 1 is just a warm up. Once your dictator has your full attention it goes in for the kill. Nothing generates more fear than a full feature film highlighting your worst nightmares. Lights. Camera. Action.

***

When we left off, Tami was in the throes of panic. She thought she could go to school but her stomach started to hurt and her confidence was faltering. But her dictator was just getting started. He has scavenged her doubts and paranoia and made a cute little home movie for her own personal enjoyment.

The movie starts in her head...

She's in the auditorium. Her stomach starts hurting. Her friends are trying to talk to her but she can't focus. She's starts to break out in a sweat. She's going to be sick. She needs to get out of there. The auditorium is completely packed. Of course she had to sit right in the middle of the row. That cute boy from algebra is sitting two seats down from her. Is it her imagination or does he keep looking over at her? Crap. She's going to be sick. She has to get to a bathroom quick. The auditorium is quiet. Everyone is focused on the stage. She stumbles and stands up. She feels the entire auditorium turn to stare at her. She tries to navigate her way down the row. She falls on people. She is almost to the aisle when it happens. She can't hold it any longer. She turns to vomit right on the lap of the cute algebra dude. He screams in disgust. *Kill me now,* she thinks. *Kill me now.*

***

We left Jon second-guessing his class presentation. He came into class with so much confidence but his dictator slowly deflated him. And, unfortunately for Jon, his dictator is not done.

Images flash in Jon's mind.

He sees the teacher insisting that he go next. He stumbles to the front of the class. His hands shake and everyone starts to laugh and point. He tries to focus on his note cards but the words are blurry as he realizes he is tearing up. Could this get more embarrassing? He berates himself and tries to push through. He stumbles over his words when the teacher jumps in. She asks him a question about his presentation. She didn't ask anyone else questions. He doesn't know how to answer her. He feels warmth crawl up his neck and settle in his cheeks. Everyone starts to laugh and whisper. He hears them whispering, "Look how red that dude is getting!" He looks in the far back and sees his only friend laughing too. How can he do that to him?

***

Amanda isn't faring much better. We left her paralyzed in bed, convinced a serial killer was waiting for her on the other side of her bedroom door. But the party is just getting started.

She can hear her heartbeat in her ears growing louder with every scene she imagines.

She visualizes the door handle being jiggled. She stops breathing as the door bursts open. She plays out her demise in slow motion. No detail is lost but I will spare you the play by play.

Step 3: Amp up the physical symptoms.

With doubt planted firmly in your head and some wonderful images to go with it, your dictator wants to now get you on your knees. Literally. He is ready to pull the alarm and set off a huge physiological reaction in your body. He wants to make you so incapacitated that you will do anything and everything to make it stop.

***

Tami has moved back to her bed. The images of her being sick have made her lose all her will to fight. She is now in the throes of pure panic. She can hear her mom walking up the stairs yelling, "Tami, we have to get going or we'll be late!" Her dictator hears this and quickly sets off the panic button. Tami instantly feels intense nausea and runs to the bathroom. Her mom shouts, "Tami, what are you doing up there?" She is on the floor of her bathroom now. She is feeling clammy and dizzy. She gags but nothing comes out.

***

Jon is overcome with fear. He has played out how his presentation will go in his mind and it wasn't good. There is no way he can go up there now! He knows he'll be called on right after the next presentation. His dictator swoops in for the kill. Alarm bells ring in Jon's mind. He can hear his heart pounding in his ears. He is having a hard time catching his breath. He's worried he's going to pass out. That would be embarrassing. The thought makes him panic even more. He can feel himself break out in a sweat. He is starting to feel sick to his stomach. His legs feel like jelly. Will he even be able to stand when he is called on? His chest is getting tight and he feels a sharp pain. Could this stress be causing him to have a heart attack? Is he going to die here in 4th period?

***

Amanda is waiting for her killer to enter the room. She is afraid to move so she remains as still as a statue. Her breathing is shallow and she is having a hard time catching her breath. She feels really hot now but she doesn't want to move the blanket off of her. For some reason she feels safer covered, even though she knows that doesn't make sense. How long can she lie like this? How long will her killer wait at her door?

***

Step 4: Scam you with solutions.

Now that your dictator has you literally on your knees, it is time for his sales pitch. This is what he has been waiting for the whole time. This is what he has been building up to—his end game. He gets stronger when you get weak. He needs you to avoid situations. He needs you to bail, to run, to leave, to give up. He will stop at nothing to convince you that this is the best option. He'll lie to you and tell you that he is looking out for your best intentions. He will make you believe that parents, relatives, friends and therapists don't understand because if they did they wouldn't force you to do the things that are causing you so much anxiety. He is a liar. A good liar. And most people are buying what he is selling. Tami, Jon and Amanda are customers. Are you?

***

Tami is exhausted. The tile feels nice and cool on her face and all she wants to do is just lie there on the floor forever—her dictator agrees! He slowly starts to offer her words of enticement.

You don't need this. You aren't going to make it anyway. Just get back into bed. Maybe you actually have a stomach virus. It is possible. Maybe you are really sick and no one will believe you. That would majorly suck. Better not chance it. Tell your mom you are seriously sick this time because maybe you are. Tell her this is not your anxiety and that you truly don't feel well. You don't need this stress; you have a true stomach condition that needs medical attention. Maybe you can be home schooled and wouldn't have to worry about whether your stomach will hurt or not. That would be nice. But first things first—call down to your mom and let her know you are truly sick. Tell her there is absolutely no way you will be going to school today and there is nothing she can do about it.

"Mom," Tami calls from her bathroom, "I think I am really sick."

***

Jon is ready to bail. He would rather die than stand up in front of his class. The nightmarish images sealed the deal for him. Now he is thinking of an exit strategy. Luckily, he has his dictator to help him!

No one should be tortured like this! No grade is worth this much stress. You have got to get out of here! Why not tell your teacher you aren't feeling well and go to the nurse? It is true, right? You don't feel well. You'd better do it soon or she's going to call on you. You are running out of time. You can't take forever to make this decision. You are going to bomb. Do you want the whole class to laugh at you? Get out of here!

Jon raises his hand. "Can I go to the nurse?"

***

Amanda has been lying quietly for over an hour, scared to death in her bed. She has convinced herself that if there was a killer at her door, he would have probably entered by now and for this reason her heart has slowed down; but she still feels very anxious. There is no way she can fall back asleep. She never gets worried when she is sleeping with her mom. For some reason she feels completely safe in her mom's room. She receives some additional encouragement from her dictator.

> *Do you want to lie here in your bed completely vulnerable?*
> *What if he is still in the house? Do you want to be in here all alone?*
> *You'll never fall back asleep. Make a run for your mom's room. I*
> *know she'll yell at you and she's told you to stay in your room, but*
> *this is your safety we are talking about!*

Amanda sits up, grabs her softball bat and plans to make a run for it.

***

Step 5: Reward you for being his compliant follower.

You have been your dictator's dutiful follower. He says, "Jump," and you say, "How high?" He likes working with you. He thinks you and he are going to get along swimmingly. He has decided to permanently move in. Get cozy. After all, he plans on being with you for the long haul. You and your dictator are going to be best buds. He's the only one who understands you, right?

He needs to reward you for your compliant behavior. He needs you to feel relief after you have blindly followed his advice.

***

The moment Tami's mom gives in and lets her stay home from school, Tami is flooded with relief. Her dictator lets the body know it was a false alarm and her stomach starts to feel better. Within an hour she is back to her regular self.

Her dictator moves in to give her reassurance that she made the right decision.

It is good you stayed home. Don't you feel better? All that pain isn't worth it. You probably feel better because you are lying down. You wouldn't be able to lie down at school.

***

Jon feels instant relief as soon as he enters the hall. The sweat starts to dry on his forehead. He heads to the nurse with a bounce in his step. *Thank goodness that is over!* His dictator wholeheartedly agrees.

You just dodged a major bullet, my friend. That would have been a complete disaster. You are not good at presentations. You just can't handle them. They should be avoided at all costs in the future.

***

Amanda is squeezed next to her mom, safely in her parents' bed. Her mom had yelled at her, but she was too tired to insist Amanda go back to her own room. She knows she'll hear about it in the morning, but it was worth it. All her worries and panic are completely gone. She isn't even thinking about whether there is someone in the house anymore. She is on her way to falling asleep. Her dictator tells her a bedtime story.

You are only safe with your mom. You can't sleep on your own. You shouldn't even try to do it tomorrow night. It is not a big deal if you sleep with your mom. It's not like you'll want to sleep with her forever. You'll outgrow this. After all, you are going to go to college next year. In the meantime, don't risk the anxiety. Just sleep with your mom. It's no big deal.

3 DEVELOPING AN ARSENAL OF WEAPONS

Now that you realize your dictator is kicking some butt, specifically your butt, it is time to start your training. If you've gotten this far in the book your training is already half way done. Say what? It's true—half the battle is knowing how your dictator works. If you know your dictator's shenanigans, they are less likely to work on you. That's good news!

You should be well aware of your dictator's pathetic moves. How your dictator 1) Picks an anxiety theme that bothers you 2) Fills you up with doubt 3) Offers you horrible visuals to go along with your worries 4) Makes you feel physically ill and 5) Convinces you to avoid whatever you fear. His actions are no longer a mystery. He is no longer a covert annoyance in your head. The gig is up, little dude.

On to the training.

Believe it or not, defeating your dictator comes down to these six deadly moves. They may not seem that lethal, but trust me; if you consistently utilize your arsenal of weapons, your dictator won't stand a chance.

So enough of this chit-chat, let's get on with it.

Move #1. Call out your dictator and let him know his ninja ways aren't working anymore.

Beating your dictator is a marathon, not a sprint. Depending on the size of your dictator, you might have your work cut out for you. Don't be naïve and think you are going to suddenly wake up without a dictator. This is going to take work. I know, not your favorite word. But trust me; the payoff is worth it and the alternative is far worse.

You want to take small steps towards annihilating your dictator. If you prematurely try to take him down, he will easily knock you back into your place. Don't be foolish. Know your limits. Small steps turn into big progress.

If you are paralyzed with anxiety, the first weapon in your arsenal should be honesty. Be honest with yourself. Don't sugarcoat and minimize the problem. Don't lie to yourself and make excuses for your worries. No, it was not because you didn't want to go to the party. No, it was not because you thought you had a stomach virus. No, it was not because you just like to be close to your mom. You have a dictator. He tells you what to do and, unfortunately, you do it.

Once you are more honest with yourself about your predicament the easier it will be to fix the problem. Remember how the dictator likes to be a silent ninja? He doesn't want you to know it is him. He wants you to make excuses for him. If you don't admit he exists, you won't be able to get rid of him. It is as simple as that.

Tell your dictator you know it is him. When you start feeling a flutter in your stomach, tell him you know he is there. When you worry that the lump on the back of your neck is a tumor, say hello to your dictator. When you worry about whether your mom has died in a car accident, thank your dictator for that morbid thought.

You might think that just recognizing your dictator is the lamest thing you've ever heard. I know it sounds lame, but I can't tell you how many kids I have worked with who couldn't get past this first step. They refused to fully acknowledge their anxiety. I have spent session after session trying to convince them that no stomach virus consistently comes on Monday and leaves on Friday, that it isn't just a "habit" to sleep with your mom or that it isn't normal to put a chair in front of your bedroom door at night.

If you aren't sure it is your dictator, ask someone who knows you well. People who get you will get your dictator too. When in doubt, ask them.

So, even if you can't beat your dictator, even if you cave and avoid whatever it is he wants you to avoid, let him know that you weren't fooled—that you never, not for a minute, thought it was anything or anyone other than him. Let him know you are studying his moves and working on a plan of attack—that he may have won that battle but he will definitely not win the war.

***

Our 3 anxious friends are going to start fighting back too...

Tami.

The next time Tami found herself lying on the bathroom floor sick to her stomach, she screamed in her mind, *I know this is you, my little dictator!*

Jon.

When Jon had another presentation later that week, he quietly waited for his dictator to arrive on the scene. He greeted him with, *I knew you would show up today!*

Amanda.

As Amanda's heart raced when she heard an unfamiliar creak in her house she had the thought, *My dictator is starting to work his magic!*

They are all calling him out and letting him know they are aware he is there.

Move #2: Don't just sit there and take his trash talk—start talking back.

Do you remember your dictator's first move? He tries to plant the seeds of doubt in your head. He is that nagging internal voice asking you a bunch of *What If* questions. What if you throw up? What if it is really cancer ... this time? What if you fail out of school and become homeless? Your dictator doesn't want you to question his *What Ifs*, he just wants you to worry about them. And most people do. But you aren't most people. You are here to kick some anxiety butt. So arm up and prepare yourself for a mind battle.

Mind bombs – Boom!

Your dictator wants you to grow his nasty thoughts. Think of it as a grenade that he smuggles into your mind. He pulls the pin and waits for it to explode. You can stop it—if you detect it soon enough and are able to throw it out of your mind or push the pin back in.

Let's take a look at mind bombs in action:

You failed the test. (Tick, tick, tick... 10)

You are going to fail this class. (9)

You are not going to pass 10th grade. (8)

You are not going to pass high school. (7)

You are going to live life without a high school diploma. (6)

You are going to have a hard time finding a job. (5)

You'll be very poor. (4)

You won't be able to pay for a house. (3)

You won't be able to pay for food. (2)

You are going to be homeless! (1)

BOOM!

This may seem drastic but I have heard this very example many times in my office. Why do we provide a stage for anxious thoughts? Why do we let these thoughts enter our minds without any observation of whether they are harmful or not?

How many times a day do we have snowball thoughts and images (yes, the dictator loves to traumatize you with visual effects)? Would you leave your home unlocked? And yet most of us leave our minds unlocked, letting anything and everything trample into our mind's eye, creating chaos in its wake.

When I tell kids they have control over what they think, they look at me like I am crazy. I tell them "Observe your thoughts. You are having some right now. Are they helping you? Hurting you? Annoying you? Would you allow someone to degrade and demean you for hours on end? But yet you let your dictator do it to you all the time."

Listen to your thoughts. You probably won't catch them right away but as you practice this you will catch them quicker. If you are having a disturbing thought, analyze it further. Ask yourself, *Is this thought helpful or hurtful?* If it is hurtful, continue your line of questioning.

Did this already happen? If so, is obsessing about the past going to help? Probably not. If it is in the past, trash it and move on. Tell yourself, *If I can't do anything about it then I am wasting my time thinking about it.* Your dictator's favorite pastime is making you feel bad about anything and everything you did in the past. Don't give him the satisfaction of giving him air time.

What if thoughts.

Ask yourself, *Is this a* What if *thought? What if* thoughts are almost never good. Why don't we ponder crap like What if *I ace that test* or What if *everyone thinks I give an awesome presentation?* No. Our dic has to give us *What ifs* like... What if *I die before I get home tonight* or What if *an asteroid hits Earth?* He sucks so badly.

So, the rule of thumb: If it is a *What If* thought, trash it and don't look back. We'll talk about how to keep thoughts in the trash in a little bit. But let's expose all of the dictator's thought tactics first.

Thought flooding.

Another tactic the dictator uses is flooding. Let's flood you with every possible worry you can have for the next ten years.

Will you have the nerve to go to that party in three weeks?

Will you do okay on that test next month?

Will you get a shot at your doctor's appointment in three months?

Will you be able to learn to drive next year?

Will you get into college in two years?

I always tell kids to imagine a stove. Your front burners are for things that are going to be happening pretty soon and your back burners are for things that will be happening in the distant future. If your dictator is trying to get you to worry about things that aren't on the front burner, you deny that sucker entry into your mind. Tell him, "Nope. Sorry, that's not happening for three more weeks. That's a back burner issue that I won't worry about for two more weeks." Giving yourself permission to worry about something later helps declutter your mind and lets you focus on the more pressing issues at hand.

Your mind is a to-do list. If a worry is supposed to be at the bottom of the list, don't let it barge it's way to the top.

Paranoid thoughts.

Along with memories of the past and future, your dictator loves to haunt you with irrational thoughts. These are harder to detect but they have a paranoid or irrational flair.

Did you put your homework in your backpack?

Are you going to die in your sleep?

What if you are not able to fall asleep—ever?

If you sit near her will you get sick too?

Do you have a disease and no one has realized it yet?

Will the world end and you'll be the only survivor?

As you can see, these thoughts are not the feel-good variety. No, doom and gloom tend to be on the menu. Ask yourself, *Does this thought rationally make sense?* The majority of paranoid thoughts will be nonsensical and irrational. Treat these thoughts with skepticism and interrogate them.

Did you put your homework in your backpack?

Yes, I literally just checked and saw it sticking out of my folder. Does it make sense that it wouldn't be there now? No. If I check it again I let the dictator fool me and I will help him grow.

Are you going to die in your sleep?

No. Why would that happen? Do kids normally just die when they go to bed? No. That is my dictator trying to fool me. I have absolutely no facts that would support that worry.

What if you are not able to fall asleep—ever?

Will my body let me go forever without sleep? No. The body will automatically shut down and get me the sleep I need. Our bodies are meant to run smoothly and have natural defenses to ensure our well-being.

If you sit near her will you get sick too?

Just because I sat near her doesn't mean I will get sick. Germs don't work that way. I didn't touch any of her things. I didn't stand close to her. I have no reason to think I will get sick just because I sat two desks behind her. I am feeling okay. I don't feel sick.

So you get the point. Argue with your dictator and provide evidence to the contrary—then trash it and move on.

Over-analyzing thoughts.

One of the dictator's favorite weapons is making you analyze things over and over again in your head, questioning and double questioning your actions, behavior and words. Nothing good ever comes out of these thoughts.

Did you hurt her feelings?

Was the teacher's comment directed at you?

When he said, "I gotta go," did you do something wrong?

Do you think everyone noticed the huge zit on your chin today?

You stumbled on your lines in the play. Do you think everyone is talking about it today?

Ask yourself, *Did this already happen?* Yes. *Is there anything I can do about it?* No. *So, is it worth thinking about?* No. Trash it. When you catch yourself having these types of thoughts, don't let them snowball into larger worries. Even if it happened two minutes ago it is still in the past.

Catch them. Destroy them. And move on.

Okay, so now you have a good idea of what type of thought grenades your dictator blows up in your mind—but how do you develop a good defense?

Develop a security system for your mind.

For starters, watch the door to your mind. Don't let just any thoughts walk in without checking them. You are the first line of defense. Think of your mind as something precious that you are trying to protect. Every thought has to walk through a thought-detector as it enters your mind. If it is a *What If* thought, a *sometime in the future* thought, a *what I did in the past* thought or an *irrational* thought your thought detector alarm should go off.

When your thought detector goes off, quickly categorize the nature of the threat.

- This is a *What if* thought—I should not talk to it. This thought does not pass the screening. In the trash it goes.

- This is a *sometime in the future* thought. Analyze the date of the impending doom. 2 years and 2 months away. Nope. Back burner it. Not getting through security.

- This is a *what I did in the past* thought. Can I change it? No. Out you go.

- This is an *irrational* thought. You gotta be kidding me. You want me to worry about an asteroid blowing up the earth? Sorry, not going to happen. You can turn yourself right around.

Unfortunately, your dictator is a determined little bugger. He doesn't give up and neither should you. He will come back in with some great disguises.

Just passing through. It's just me, a nostalgic thought. Totally innocent.

But once through the dictator rears its ugly head.

Remember when you used to hang out with Tom. He was so much fun. *(Innocent* thought*)*

Too bad he doesn't talk to you anymore. (*Uh-oh we are going south* thought)

I wonder what you did to upset him. *(*The dictator comes on the scene with a *What I did in the past* thought*)*

Be aware. Don't be suckered into a mind bomb because you didn't keep your guard up. If a thought is suddenly making you feel anxious or bad about yourself, quickly send security to kick it out of your head.

Make sure negative thoughts are productive.

That is not to say that you can't allow yourself to have some unpleasant thoughts. The mind is a great way to process your emotions and learn from your past mistakes. The key word is **learn**. If you are not gaining any insight or knowledge into your behavior you are empowering your dictator.

Healthy thoughts might go something like this:

Mary didn't say a word to me today.

I wonder if she is mad at me.

Actually she didn't say a word to anyone.

She did mention that her mom was in the hospital.

I should ask her how her mom is doing tomorrow.

This is a healthy internal dialogue about a friend's behavior and a helpful conclusion. The trick is to know the difference and to catch it when it is going in the wrong direction.

For instance:

Mary didn't say a word to me today.

I wonder if she is mad at me.

I never understood why she liked me anyway.

She's so pretty and popular and I'm such a dork.

She's probably embarrassed by me.

I should stop talking to her and do us both a favor!

As you can see, these two thoughts created very different conclusions, conclusions that could ruin a friendship for no good reason or encourage you to reach out and be a kind friend.

Prepare for a battle of wills.

So, I've been telling you to "trash" bad thoughts. I get that it is not that simple. I have my own dictator that I have been silencing for decades—so, yeah, I get how persistent and convincing he can be at times. That is why you need to prepare for battle and not give up.

Once you detect a mind bomb call in your thought security. Assess the risk. What kind of thought is this—a *What if* thought, a *leave it in the past* thought? Arm up your troops and recognize that you have a thought battle on your hands. I like to call the dictator's thoughts "red thoughts" (because I am weird). For every red thought he throws at you, you have to throw one of your rational green thoughts (yes, the weirdness continues) back.

For example:

What if the pain in your leg is really a tumor?

Ah, a *What if* thought—this can't be good.

No, seriously, what if that bump is a tumor?

What bump?

That slightly raised skin on your leg.

You are not suckering me into thinking about this!

What if you get really sick?

I am perfectly healthy. I just had a checkup last week.

What if you didn't have it last week?

Bye-bye, *What if* thought. Bye-bye, Dictator. I am no longer giving you my attention!

Your first line of defense is to acknowledge that you are being thought bombed. Second—figure out what type of thought is trying to come through. Last—you will have to throw rational, fact-oriented green thoughts back at the thought bomb. If you don't fight back and just try to distract yourself the bomb will eventually go off. If you have a hard time generating green thoughts, ask someone who is close to you. Some people are good at coming up with green thoughts and some people come up empty.

Once you have successfully defused the thought bomb you'll need to quickly distract yourself. Don't just stand there waiting for your dictator to throw another thought bomb your way. Get moving.

The art of distraction.

People with anxiety do not always understand how to use distraction and yet every person with anxiety uses it. If you just try to distract yourself—without throwing green thoughts back—all you are doing is delaying when your thought bomb will go off. It will eventually go off.

No, instead you need to learn how to get at the heart of the thought. Stare down the enemy and diffuse the thought bomb. And *then* distract yourself.

I understand that there will be times when this is not possible. There will be times when you are on the verge of panic and cannot fight at all. When you are in these situations you can still recognize the type of thought bomb being thrown your way—you just might not have the energy to throw back green thoughts. When you are in this type of crisis, go to distraction quick, fast and in a hurry. It just can't be your only plan of attack all of the time.

When using distraction—whether after a good battle or when using it as an emergency escape plan—make sure it fully consumes your attention.

Often, when I ask kids what they use to distract themselves they will say things like music or drawing. I don't know about you, but I have the ability to listen to music *and* worry. I can also draw and worry. I can actually do most passive activities and worry and I bet you can too.

You want to find an activity that requires more concentration and focus. I can't read and worry. I can read a page, zone out and worry, and then realize I skipped a page. But I can't do both at the exact same time.

I always tell people to make a short list of maybe five activities that are their go-to distraction weapons. It is good to identify what these are ahead of time because when you are frazzled by thought bombs you aren't going to be able to come up with them. They have to work for you and everyone is different. What might work for me might not work for you and vice versa.

Here are some examples of good distractions but you may have your own already:

- Text a friend (typing and worrying at the same time can be tricky)

- Have a conversation with someone (not about the worry though)

- Watch TV

- Read a book

- Play a video game (you can tell your parents I said it was therapeutic. You're welcome)

- Watch YouTube

- Play an instrument

- Play a word game (simple word games keep the mind busy. Go through the alphabet and find something in the room that begins with each letter of the alphabet—that will bore your brain into submission)

Imagery is another distraction weapon that is good to put in your arsenal of defense tactics. This is best to use when you think you are *going to be* anxious but aren't already in that state of mind. Kind of like a preemptive strike.

Create a world in your mind. This is best done when you are relaxed and aren't doing it out of necessity. You want it to be a simple world with no story line. This is not a world with lots of characters and plot twists. Pick a place. Is it a fantasy world with dragons or do you like a forest scene? I have heard everything from a candy land world to a Star Wars world. Pick something you love and go from there.

What's in your world? I love off the wall, magical elements in my world. What does your world smell like? Sound like? Feel like? What can you do in your world? You want to have some activities to keep your mind somewhat engaged.

Once you have your world created, try to avoid continually changing the theme. The more you mentally visit the same world over and over again the more real it will become in your imagination. When your world is very real, it will be easier to enter that world to use it as a distraction.

I have used my world for decades. If I am having trouble sleeping, off to my world I go. If I have to give blood I turn the other way and think of my world. Using a world as a distraction or to go to sleep can be super helpful.

***

Tami.

Tami is no longer in denial. She knows her dictator is getting the best of her. She knows she doesn't have some undiagnosed medical issue with her stomach. Her issue is her dictator and she intends to kick his butt and get back her life.

She is almost out the door to go to school when her dictator throws a mind bomb and starts a false alarm throughout her body. Nausea hits her like a ton of bricks.

You can't do this! You are sick. You won't make it through the day!

She calls out her dictator:

I know those are your mind bombs, dictator—and I am not going to let you win this time!

Don't you see how nauseous you feel?

I am not going to let any more of your thoughts get through, sucker!

She throws back green thought bombs:

I can do this!

I may feel queasy, but I always feel better after the first half of the school day.

If I work through this I can get rid of this problem forever!

The more I give my nausea attention the more it will grow.

She ends with distraction:

I am done with giving you my full attention. I am turning your channel in my mind off. I am going to watch my favorite show while I get ready for school—that way you won't have a channel to present me with your red thought ideas. Sayonara.

Jon.

Jon is in class when the girl next to him asks if he can tell her the homework assignment. His dictator quickly answers for him.

No, you can't. The minute you open up your mouth you are going to sound stupid.

Just act like you didn't hear her.

Don't look up.

He calls out his dictator:

Little dictator, I always let you ruin things for me.

You sabotage everything.

He throws green thought bombs:

This is my chance to talk to that girl.

All she wants is the homework, I *can* do that.

It will be worse if I don't say anything.

He ends with distraction:

I will focus on answering her and looking at my paper for the assignment.

Amanda.

Amanda knows her anxiety is ruining her sleep. She worries about bad things happening all the time but sleep is the worst. She can't live like this much longer. She feels as though she walks around like a zombie all day. She lies in bed and so it begins again...

Everyone is already asleep but you.

You are pretty much in this house by yourself.

Someone could come in and kill you and no one would know.

She calls out her dictator:

You show up every night and give me these horrible thoughts!

I am sick of it!

She throws green thought bombs:

I am safe.

All the doors are locked.

I am not alone; my parents are right down the hall.

She ends with distraction:

I will think of the world I created in my mind. If that doesn't work, I will go through the alphabet and come up with a word for each letter. That will bore my dictator!

Move #3: Don't be fooled by false alarms in your body.

As we talked about earlier, your dictator loves to pull the emergency alarm in your brain. It is actually one of his most effective and deadliest weapons. It can stop you dead in your tracks. So, how do you fight back?

Recognize false alarms for what they are—false.

For starters, educate yourself. Understand how your dictator can impact your physical well-being. We went over this in the first chapter. Realize that the following symptoms can coincide with anxiety:

- Stomachaches

- Nausea

- Shortness of breath

- Racing heart

- Chest pain

- Lightheadedness

- Dizziness

- Dry mouth

- Difficulty swallowing

- Lump in the throat

- Weakness

- Fatigue

- Headaches

- Constipation

- Diarrhea

That's a pretty long list of physical symptoms that the dictator has at his disposal. Totally not fair. When you have any of these symptoms, ask yourself, *What is happening now or in the next 24 hours that the dictator might be quietly trying to sabotage?* Is it a school night? A day before a presentation? A few hours before going to a new class? Bedtime?

The majority of people I see will deny that these physical symptoms have anything to do with anxiety—and the dictator likes it that way. Even after doctors have cleared people of any medical origin, even when they are ridden with anxiety, they will choose to remain in denial and believe it is solely a medical issue.

Perhaps it is because it is easier to deal with a medical origin that you have no part in fixing. Perhaps the burden of it being "psychological" places blame on the patient. It shouldn't. The pain is real—you are not making that up. The good news is that you can play a role in alleviating your symptoms. That is not bad news—that's awesome. It is not some medical mystery that will leave you debilitated for years. It's your dictator. And the sooner you defeat him the sooner your physical symptoms will go away.

There are three ways physical symptoms arrive on the scene.

They can be **ongoing symptoms** that you are continually struggling with—such as headaches, stomachaches or constipation.

They can be **sudden physical symptoms** like those associated with an anxiety attack [anxiety caused by a stressor]—such as shortness of breath and dry mouth.

Or they can be more **extreme physical symptoms** like those associated with a panic attack [acute anxiety that can happen randomly, without a stressor]—such as chest pain, heart palpitations and difficulty breathing.

The key to overcoming false alarms is to realize that they are just that—false! Ask yourself these questions to help you recognize the dictator's handiwork:

Am I nervous about something that is happening or will be happening that could be causing my physical symptoms?

Often people get physically sick with worry but aren't even aware that they are nervous. Your dictator is a shifty dude. He likes to slip past your conscious awareness and slip under your radar.

If I left the current situation would I feel better?

Imagine leaving or not doing the thing you are supposed to be doing. Do you start to feel better?

Have I had these feelings before and everything turned out to be okay?

Do you get nauseous often? Do you get stress headaches? Are these normally fleeting feelings that go away after a little while?

Are all my symptoms also symptoms of anxiety?

Do your symptoms all coincide with physical symptoms of anxiety?

Demystify panic attacks.

Panic attacks deserve some of their own attention. A panic attack is a false alarm that doesn't have to be triggered by any external stress. That is where your dictator really gets you. He reminds you that you are not doing anything anxiety producing, therefore you must be having a true medical emergency. This makes you panic even more and, voilà, a full-blown panic attack is born.

Arm yourself with these facts and beat him at his own game:

- I don't need to be stressed to have a panic attack.

- I don't need to be anxious to have a panic attack.

- A panic attack is a misfire in my body. A false alarm.

- People don't die or get injured from the physical symptoms of a panic attack.

Panic attack symptoms can include heart pain and palpitations, chest pain, shortness of breath, shallow breathing, dry mouth and feelings of not being real or being outside of one's self.

Keep a panic attack journal and write down what physical symptoms you experience and how long they last. When you are having a panic attack, read your journal and remind yourself that these are symptoms of a panic attack.

Do not let your dictator pass your mind's security and enter your thoughts.

Once you have correctly identified that you are having a false alarm the mind battle should commence. Most people move to distraction and forget this key step. Your distraction will be much more effective if you tackle some mind bombs first.

Your dictator is hoping you never realize your physical symptoms are him wreaking havoc on your body. He is hoping that he can bring you to your knees without too much effort on his part. Show him he is wrong.

Your dictator is throwing only one red thought bomb at you—*You are sick!* Throw these green thought bombs back at him:

I am not sick. I am having anxiety (or a panic attack).

My pain is real but it is the dictator not an illness.

This will pass—as it always does.

The more I worry about this the sicker I will feel.

The less I focus on these symptoms the quicker the pain will go away.

If I avoid activities that cause me anxiety, these false alarms will happen more often.

Have 5 go-to things that make you feel better when having a false alarm.

Now that you know it is a false alarm and you have blocked your dictator's red thought bombs and counterattacked with your green thought bombs, bring on the distraction. Find 5 go-to things that are your best distraction weapons. As we talked about before, these will be different for everyone. Play around with methods of distraction until you find the right one for you. For panic attacks, adding physical distractions along with mental distractions can be helpful. Your body is being flooded with adrenaline and cortisol and could benefit from a physical activity to work some of that off.

Let's see how our 3 friends are coping with their physical distress:

Tami.

When we left Tami she was angry and ready to fight this beast. She was counterattacking her dictator's red thought bombs with her green ones. Let's see how she deals with his deadliest weapon:

The dictator throws a physical attack at her stomach. This always works. She should be relenting and caving to his demands at any moment.

She recognizes that she is having a false alarm:

Tami wants to puke. She knows this feeling. She has this feeling every morning before school. She also knows that this is what a false alarm feels like in her body.

<u>She counterattacks with green thought bombs:</u>

Yes, the nausea is real but I am strong.

I can work through this.

If I just hold it together I can ride through this pain and the dictator will lose his power.

<u>She moves into distraction:</u>

I am going to watch TV and get my mind off this pain and the dictator.

Jon.

Jon is starting to have a physical reaction to the stress brought on by his classmate talking to him. His mouth is going dry and his heart is pounding in his ears. He is starting to feel panicky. What if he gets sick or can't speak?

<u>He recognizes that he is having a false alarm:</u>

Jon reminds himself that this is how he feels when he is nervous—that this is the dictator's handiwork. He isn't going to be sick because, once he counterattacks, he is going to win.

<u>He counterattacks with green thought bombs:</u>

I've got this.

If I just answer her, these physical symptoms will go away and I won't feel sick.

<u>He quickly moves his focus and attention:</u>

Answer her and move on.

Amanda

Amanda's heart is pounding in her chest. She is starting to feel weak. She has a weird feeling as though she can't move one muscle or the imaginary bad guy will know she is awake. Her body is starting to feel tense from staying in one position for too long.

<u>She recognizes that she is having a false alarm:</u>

My body is reacting as if there is a crisis. The only crisis is the one in my head. Once I realize I am safe, these physical warning signs that I am in danger will go away.

<u>She counterattacks with green thought bombs:</u>

I am safe.

There are no real signs that I am in danger.

I am not alone. My whole family is home with me.

<u>She quickly moves to distract herself:</u>

I am going to think of my world or play the alphabet game.

Move #4: Remove your dictator's double agents.

Your dictator can control you because he has worked very hard to infiltrate your beliefs. He has sent his double agents to alter the way you think. If they can convince you that you are having these thoughts there will be no need to exert any energy in thought bombing or setting off false alarms.

Double agents use the following three tactics. Learn them. Expose them. Change them.

"I can't" beliefs.

I can't tell you how many people I have worked with who speak the language of "I can't." Your dictator's double agents have done an amazing job at convincing you of your limits. You have eagerly believed them and have incorporated these beliefs into your own thoughts.

I can't do presentations

I can't eat in the cafeteria

I can't sleep over at other people's houses

I can't be left alone at home

I can't be in crowds

I can't fly

Yes, you can! It may be hard. It may be scary. But technically you can do it. When you speak the language of *I can't* you have already given up. You have set false limitations on yourself that you are not likely to break.

Change the way you think and weaken your dictator and his double agents.

I can do presentations. I don't enjoy them but I technically can do them.

I can eat in the cafeteria. I don't like the smell of food but there are ways I can deal with it.

I can have sleepovers at other people's homes. I just need to find ways to make me feel comfortable.

I can be left at home alone. When I lock all the doors and have my phone with me, I can feel safe.

I can be in crowds. If I stay by a door, I will feel less claustrophobic.

I can fly. When I bring lots of distractions I can make it through a flight.

When your thoughts leave some wiggle room for change you have a better chance of beating your dictator. You may not want to do a presentation any time soon but you know you *could* do it.

"It's a habit" beliefs,

The other common excuse I hear is, "It's a habit." Your dictator's double agents have convinced you that some of your anxious behaviors are really just habits or behaviors that you *choose to do*. Don't buy what they are selling! When you call your anxious behaviors habits, you are never going to change them!

Don't tell yourself:

It is just a habit that I wash my hands all the time.

It is just a habit that I do my evening routine in the exact same order.

It is just a habit that my mom has to say the same exact phrase when putting me to bed.

It is just a habit that I have to check and re-check the locks before I go to bed.

It is just a habit that I need to always know where my mom is at all times.

Recognize your anxious behavior for what it is—anxious behavior. When you change your perception of these behaviors, you will finally have a chance to change them and weaken your dictator.

I don't need to wash my hands all the time. My dictator tells me I need to but I don't.

If I did my evening routine in a different order, it would still be alright.

My mom doesn't have to say, "I love you," in a certain way before I go to bed.

I don't have to re-check everything. One check is good enough.

I don't have to know where my mom is all the time.

Don't lie to yourself and believe your behaviors are habits. Be honest with yourself. It doesn't mean that you have to give up these behaviors overnight but it does mean that you realize they are the dictator's habits—not yours.

"I have a reason..." beliefs.

I have heard some pretty creative excuses in my therapy practice. The dictator's double agents love to provide you with excuses to avoid anxiety-producing situations. If you believe the excuses they provide, the dictator doesn't have to use mind bombs or false alarms on you. This is much easier on him and a sign that you are working on the same team. Don't be on his team!

Do any of these excuses sound familiar?

I don't want to do it because I am lazy.

I don't want to go because it doesn't sound fun.

I can't do it because I am super busy.

I can't do it; I don't think my parents will let me go.

I can't go, I am not feeling well.

When you believe their excuses, you will remain in your dictator's grip forever. And no one reading this book wants to do that— right? Be honest with yourself and strip away his lies.

I don't want to do it because I am nervous.

I don't want to go because meeting new people is overwhelming.

I don't want to do it because it makes me anxious.

I don't want to do it because I am worried.

I don't want to go because my dictator is making me feel sick.

Honesty is the first step in making a change.

***

Tami.

Tami realized that she used to have an *"I have a reason"* belief:

I get sick in the mornings because I have a serious stomach condition. I can't go to school because I am sick, not because I am nervous.

She now knows those are false beliefs. She now believes:

My dictator causes my stomach to hurt on school days. The pain is real but I do not have a serious stomach condition. I have a serious dictator condition. The more I avoid school the bigger my dictator problem will become.

Jon.

Jon now recognizes that he used to have an *"I can't"* belief:

I can't talk to people because I am shy and people don't like me.

He now believes:

I avoid people because my dictator makes me think people don't like me. But the more I ignore people the likelier that will be.

Amanda.

Amanda used to have an *"It's a habit"* belief:

I stay up at night because it's a habit. I am not a good sleeper.

Amanda now believes:

My dictator convinces me I am not safe at night. I avoid sleep because I am scared.

Move #5: Do the opposite of what your dictator wants you to do.

You are moving along. You now know most of the dictator's tricks. They are simple but crippling. You have been on the defensive this whole time—detecting attacks and counterattacking. It is now time for you to go on the offensive. Make the first move. Rattle the cage.

These last two moves are your moves—not the dictator's. This is what is going to move you from being a victim to being a fighter.

We have learned that the dictator convinces you to do something. Mostly he wants you to avoid but he can convince you to do other things as well, such as check and double check and a whole bunch of other dictatorish, nonsensical behavior.

When your dictator tells you to do or not do something it is for **his** benefit not yours. You might feel like it is what you want as well—but we now know that is not true.

The best way to dominate your dictator is to do THE OPPOSITE of what he wants you to do. If he wants you to avoid something then you do it. If he wants you to re-check something then you don't. If he wants you to call your mom one more time you don't.

You show your dictator who is boss. He doesn't own you. He doesn't tell you what to do. You are tired of his excuses. You are tired of his games. If it is something you have to do then you'll do it. You'll go to school. You'll talk to people. If it is something you don't have to do and it doesn't make sense you won't do it. You are not going to check if your homework is in your bag for the 100th time. You are not going to cut your food into a zillion tiny bites so you don't choke. No, you are going to start living life for YOU, not for him.

This move isn't going to be easy. The next one won't be either—but these are the killer moves, the ones that, with practice, will obliterate your dictator. There will be days when you won't be able to do this, days where you are just too weak to fight. That's okay. You don't have to win every battle to win the war. Don't turn on yourself and tear yourself down when you lose a battle. You have enough enemies fighting within you—don't join their team.

Be your best supporter and cheerleader. Encourage yourself. Tell yourself *It's okay. You can fight this battle again tomorrow. Every day is a new day.*

The dictator is at his strongest when you are tired, exhausted or sick. He also likes to attack when you are already overwhelmed with external stress (like school work or family issues). Battles during those times may not be won at first—and that's okay. Allow failures to happen without giving yourself a mental beating. Every day should be a blank slate.

***

Tami, Jon and Amanda are starting to get their groove. They now know how the dictator works and realize it is surprisingly simplistic. They have started counterattacking his beliefs and they are ready to make their first offensive move.

Tami.

Tami's dictator loves that she doesn't go to school. She now understands that the more she avoids school the stronger her dictator becomes. Although her dictator mind bombs her and triggers a horrible false alarm in her body, she is going to go to school. She will win that battle.

She is going to outsmart her dictator. Her school has agreed to allow her to go to the nurse whenever she is having a false alarm. The dictator can no longer scare her with thoughts of:

Where will you go when you are sick?

Everyone is going to see you throw up!

You should just stay home!

She has a plan of her own.

I will go to the nurse when I am sick.

No one will see me throw up.

When I feel better I can go back to class. There will be no rush.

I will go to school and win the battle.

Jon.

Jon's dictator is very content with his social avoidance. As long as Jon isolates and feels overwhelmed, his dictator can convince him that people don't like him.

Jon doesn't like feeling this way. He wants to be able to talk to other people. He doesn't want a ton of friends but he'd love a best friend, someone who gets him. He'd love someone to eat lunch with and hang out with after school. His dictator has been ruining this for him.

Jon knows that if he started talking to a few people he'd gain some confidence. But just the thought of it makes his dictator fill his mind with horrible images. He decides that the next time someone starts a conversation with him, he'll respond differently. He won't try to end the conversation. He'll be friendly and do the opposite of what the dictator tells him.

Amanda

Amanda is tired. She is tired of being tired. Her dictator has her up late into the night preparing for an attack that never comes. She wants to just relax and fall asleep like everyone else. Her dictator wants her to avoid sleep. Her dictator wants her to cave and go to her mom's room.

Not anymore.

Amanda started coming up with a plan. She started to alter her room to feel safer at night. She never liked her bed by the window so she had her dad help her move it. She didn't like the way there were slits in her blinds, so her parents got her curtains. She thought her old dolls were creepy at night, so she boxed them up and put them in the garage. Her lamp by the bed created large shadows in her room, so she got a better nighttime light that lit up her room. She was tired of over analyzing every noise at night, so her mom downloaded some soothing guided imagery that she could listen to as she went to sleep.

She was tired of being a victim every night. She was tired of letting her dictator rule her thoughts and fears. From now on she was in charge.

Move #6: Seek out situations your dictator wants you to avoid.

And now for the grand finale. Be warned, this is the hardest move yet. You have fine-tuned the art of doing the opposite of what your dictator wants but that's not enough. Once you are winning most of your battles it is time to up your game. Purposely seek out situations that once would make you nervous. Don't let life just happen—seek it out. The more practice you have tackling your dictator the weaker he becomes. So why not create more battles?

Be warned, this isn't for the fainthearted. This will take courage— lots of it. This is the last step for a reason. Don't skip and go to this step before you have mostly mastered the previous five moves. You want to feel successful, not discouraged.

So ask yourself, *What situations make my dictator salivate? What situations give me false alarms?* Those are the situations you need to seek out. Go to the battle zone—don't let the battle zone come to you.

The more you expose yourself to situations where the dictator makes you feel uncomfortable the less power he will have over you.

Does the dictator make you hate crowds?

Find a crowd and use your coping mechanisms.

Does the dictator make you hate germs?

Walk around a hospital.

Does the dictator make you afraid to stay home alone?

Stay home alone.

Does the dictator make you fear talking to strangers?

Purposely start a conversation with a waitress or cashier.

These battles are twice as powerful because you initiated them. You controlled the situation and you decided to take your dictator on. This will catch your dictator off guard and will give you the upper hand.

You don't have to love doing these things—you just have to get through them. The more you do them the less power your dictator will have over you.

***

Tami.

Tami was tired of running from her dictator. She stopped avoiding school and, surprisingly, her stomach eventually stopped hurting as much. Mornings went much smoother. Knowing she could go to the nurse if she needed to seemed to take away some of her stress. She still had her rough days but she was getting through them.

Tami noticed that, although she was able to go to school, she didn't like going out on the weekends. Her dictator made her worry that maybe she would throw up when she was out in public or have a panic attack. She didn't like going to restaurants for fear that the smells might make her nauseous and she would throw up.

Tami was excited about the progress she had made and she wasn't about to let her dictator gain any more power. She wanted to take him down. She made an agreement with her parents that they would go out to eat at least once a week in spite of her dictator's discouragement.

Jon.

Jon was also tired of his dictator. He started talking to the guy who sat next to him in geometry and he found out they had a lot in common. They weren't best friends yet but he was a friendly face in 4th period and that made a huge difference to Jon. Jon began to realize that his dictator kept him isolated and by doing so closed off any opportunities for friendships.

Jon was sticking to his new rule of talking to anyone who started a conversation with him but what if he took it to the next level? What if he forced himself to initiate a conversation? There was a girl in his 2nd period class who always smiled at him and had tried to talk to him in the past. He made a pact with himself that he would talk to her. Not a huge conversation but he would ask to borrow a pencil.

Amanda.

Amanda has been kicking some butt at night. The changes in her room have helped and the distraction of the audiobook really helps. She has her bad nights, but most nights she falls asleep much quicker than in the past.

Amanda wants to keep up with her success, so she has asked her parents if they can leave her home alone during the day, once a week, for an hour. They have agreed. She looks at the challenge as a weekly battle she takes on with her dictator. Every week she feels him getting smaller and smaller.

4 FINISH HIM!

You are armed to the hilt. You know your dictator's games and you aren't playing anymore. You even set up your own battles once in a while. That is awesome. So are we done? Not quite. I need to cover just a few more things.

You will win some battles and lose others.

It is important not to get ahead of yourself. As I talked about before, you are going to win some battles and lose others. If you let your losses get the best of you your dictator will take advantage of the situation and will get the upper hand.

Big progress comes from small victories. Consistency is key. Winning large battles once in a while is less effective than winning small victories every day. Take small steps to conquer your dictator. Victories can be anything from just recognizing it is your dictator all the way to purposely putting yourself in anxiety-producing situations. Every step is vital. Every step is significant. If you can just call out your dictator you are doing something more than nothing.

Some people in your life may not get this. They may not see your internal fight or the mental steps you are taking to fight your dictator. That's okay, this isn't about them. They may not understand the struggle or the moves you are making to win battles. They might just see your outward behavior, which for a while won't look that much different. It is not until you get to the later moves that other people will start recognizing your progress.

Fight your dictator for you, not for other people.

You can't get rid of the dictator but you can take away his power.

I have a slightly disappointing tidbit to tell you. No matter how awesome your mad skills become, your dictator might still hang around. Like we talked about at the beginning of this book, dictators run in families and there is a genetic component that can be hard to completely erase.

But the good news is that, instead of being a huge dictator, he will become an annoying flea. A flea that you can barely hear. A flea that tries to upset you but fails miserably.

Don't get upset if you hear the flea. It doesn't mean your dictator is coming back or that you did something wrong. Just push him away with your killer moves and he'll have no chance with you.

The power of the dictator may also be cyclical. This means you might have periods in your life when he is really strong and periods when he is really weak. This happens due to many circumstances. Dictators thrive during change, transitions and life stressors. They also like it when you are exhausted, overworked and malnourished. Don't get discouraged when your dictator gains some momentum, it just means you have to utilize your moves and shrink him back to a smaller size. You've got this.

Find ways to de-stress, the dictator feeds off stress.

Since you know that the dictator gains power when you have life stressors, it is important to come up with an ongoing plan for how to de-stress. That means, for starters, you need to get tuned into your body and your mind. Learn the early warning signs of stress so you can act quickly to reduce it. What makes you feel relaxed? Here are some obvious ones but, as with everything, different things work for different people.

Consider whether you feel relaxed when you...

- Talk with friends

- Take a bath

- Play video games

- Write or journal

- Watch TV or YouTube

- Draw

- Read

- Listen to music

- Write music

- Play an instrument

- Write poetry

- Exercise

- Run

- Do photography

- Bike ride

- Skate

- Go to the mall

- Do your nails

- Build something

- Cook

- Do a craft

Find your thing or things and do it. Do it often. Stress. Relax. Stress. Repeat.

If you don't take care of yourself your dictator will and you don't want that to happen.

Avoid creating stress for yourself. I have seen way too many procrastinators in my therapy practice. This is a form of avoiding and is not helpful in the long run. If you put things off because you don't want to deal with them, you might want to change this habit. This is the worst habit for people with a small dictator within them. Your dictator will capitalize on your crunch time and will make you feel more than a bit overwhelmed.

If you are one of those people who think they can take on the world, you might want to slow down a bit—or at least prioritize. Don't over schedule yourself and don't spread yourself out too thin. You don't have to be everything to everyone. Learn to let things go. Learn to say no. Be realistic with what you can and can't do. If you see things piling on, know when you have to cut something loose or lower your expectations. Work smarter not harder.

Along with handling your stress, watch your sleep and diet as well. Some people may be able to pull an all-nighter but you are not one of them. When you lack sleep your dictator can get louder and more annoying. Word of advice—sleep. Don't be a vampire.

Okay, here is the section where I lecture you about your diet. Blah, blah, blah—I know. But, seriously, there a few things you should definitely know. For starters, caffeine is absolutely not your friend. Caffeine can make your body feel jittery, which can cause more false alarms to happen. If you aren't sure, experiment with caffeine and see how it affects your body.

So, if caffeine is not your friend, energy drinks are your absolute enemies. Energy drinks contain tons of caffeine and sugar (both of which are not good for those housing a dictator). Avoid energy drinks at all costs; they can seriously set you back.

So those are the absolute no-nos. I should also quickly mention—even though I am seriously trying not to be preachy—that drugs are not only bad in general but especially bad for those with dictators. You think you have paranoia and disturbing thoughts when you are not on drugs; you don't even want to hear your thoughts when you are on drugs. It is not pretty and should be avoided at all costs. Drugs also have long lasting effects on dictators that you may not notice when you are high. Drugs are like a supercharge for your dictator—so even if you don't get paranoid thoughts when you are using drugs, the power of your dictator will double for the long term.

There are some foods that have been known to help get rid of dictators. They aren't going to do your fighting for you but every little bit helps, right?

Here is a quick sample of some foods that can help:

- Oatmeal

- Bread

- Pasta

- Fruits

- Vegetables

- Walnuts

- Soybeans

- Edamame

- Sunflower seeds

- Potatoes

- Turkey

- Bananas

- Eggs

You want to look for foods high in protein. As I said before, sugar is not helpful so avoid sugary foods. Some supplements have been known to have a positive effect on killing dictators. They include magnesium, omega three fatty acids and Vitamin D and B complex. There has been research that shows probiotics and fermented foods help keep the digestive tract healthy—which has been linked to dictatorships. I am not a dietician and this is just a sample to get you thinking about your diet. I would recommend reading *The Anti-Anxiety Food Solution* by Trudy Scott for a wealth of knowledge in this area.

Meet some of the dictator's relatives.

We are wrapping up this little talk but I have to discuss one more thing. The dictator has relatives. It's true. I hope you haven't met any of them but I should give you the low down about who they are and how they operate. Unfortunately, if you have a dictator, you are more likely to meet his relatives as well. It doesn't mean you will, it just means the odds are a bit higher. The dictator likes to hang out with his relatives.

OCD.

People with dictators are more likely to get a visit from OCD as well. OCD is much like his relative the dictator but he likes you to be more of a servant for him. He makes up weird rules and makes you feel you have to do them. The dictator and OCD often have similar themes but it is their tactics that differ. For example:

The dictator might make you worry about germs but OCD will make you wash your hands every time you worry.

The dictator might make you worry about your safety but OCD might tell you to tap three times and everyone will be okay. OCD makes no rational sense but it doesn't matter. You'll still do it.

The dictator might make you worry that you'll throw up but OCD will convince you that you need to wear a particular outfit every single day to guarantee you won't be sick.

OCD is your dictator's nasty cousin. He deserves a book of his own.

Trichotillomania.

Trichotillomania is a fancy name for hair pulling. The same part of the brain that houses your annoying little dictator and his nasty cousin OCD also houses Trichotillomania.

Trichotillomania is an intense desire to pull your hair out. He can target your eyebrows, eyelashes and hair—or all three. Many people don't know that Trich is related to your dictator and OCD but they are buddies and tend to travel together.

Picking

Pick lives with Trich, OCD and your dictator. He likes to make you obsessively pick your scabs until they bleed and scar. He is unrelenting and harmful to your skin and health.

Those are the main relatives that you need to keep your eye out for—but hopefully you'll never meet them.

5 CONCLUSION

It appears we have come to the end, my friend. I have taught you all I know. The student shall now become the master. As you can see, understanding your dictator is really not that hard. The challenge is in the battles. His weapons may be simplistic but they are effective. He has been fine tuning his skills for years and you are new to the game. Heck, you didn't even know you needed to show up for the battle when we first met.

Give yourself some time and be patient. As I said before, success is achieved one small step at a time. Celebrate your small wins. Don't be your own worst critic. Most importantly, get support. You don't have to do this alone. Find a support system. Preferably an adult. Your friends have their own issues.

I have worked with so many teens who solely rely on their friends to help their anxiety or depression. This can be a slippery slope as sometimes you both get worse. I have seen this time and time again.

When someone is drowning, you don't jump in with them—you throw them a life saver. Your friends can't throw you a life saver when they are swimming with you.

Confide in your parent or another trusted adult. Don't be afraid to go to a therapist. A therapist can help you use the tools I taught you and can help you fine-tune them. Everyone's anxiety is different and this book is just a general guide on how to beat it. Your therapist can help give you individualized suggestions and can help you work through your struggles when you hit a snag.

It's been fun but our journey has ended. I wish you the best in your battles, dictator slayer. You are more awesome than you think.

ABOUT THE AUTHOR

Natasha Daniels lives with her husband and three children in Phoenix, Arizona. When she is not working in her therapy practice she is writing for her parenting website AnxiousToddlers.com.

She can be reached at info@anxioustoddlers.com

Made in the USA
Lexington, KY
24 August 2019